THE BRAIN WORKOUT

Dr Gareth Moore is the author of a wide range of brain-training and puzzle books for both children and adults, including *Train the Brain* and *The 10-Minute Brain Workout*. His brain training material has also appeared in a wide range of newspapers and magazines.

He writes and runs the monthly logic puzzle magazine *Sudoku Xtra*, as well as the popular online puzzle site *PuzzleMix.com*. He gained his Ph.D at the University of Cambridge, UK, where he taught machines to recognize the English language.

THE BRAIN
WORKOUT

USE IT *OR* LOSE IT

DR GARETH MOORE

Michael O'Mara Books Limited

First published in Great Britain in 2011 by
Michael O'Mara Books Limited
9 Lion Yard
Tremadoc Road
London SW4 7NQ

A CIP catalogue record for this book is available
from the British Library.

Papers used by Michael O'Mara Books Limited are natural, recyclable
products made from wood grown in sustainable forests. The
manufacturing processes conform to the environmental regulations of
the country of origin.

ISBN: 978-1-84317-563-6

3 5 7 9 10 8 6 4 2

www.mombooks.com

www.drgarethmoore.com

Typeset and designed by Gareth Moore

Printed and bound by CPI Group (UK) Ltd,
Croydon, CR0 4YY

CONTENTS

INTRODUCTION

Your brain governs every part of your body, from conscious thought to unconscious breath, so looking after it is just as critical to your body's overall health as keeping physically fit.

Despite accounting for only 2% of your body weight, your brain requires 20% of all of the energy you use. Unlike the rest of your body, it uses almost as much energy when asleep as awake, as it busily files and tidies away the mental deductions and observations of the day. This is why ensuring adequate sleep is essential for good mental health, and having a ready supply of energy for your brain is important. If you're physically unfit then your heart can't pump energy-bearing blood to your brain quickly enough and so your thinking slows down.

Your brain loves novelty – new experiences, new feelings, new thoughts – so challenge yourself and try out new things. Travel as widely as you can, and seek out trickier problems at work, school or home. However, most of us don't have these options every day, and that's where this book comes in – it's packed full of novel and interesting challenges to exercise your cerebral cortex, the uppermost part of your brain that governs all of your conscious thoughts and actions. And you'll have fun too!

Brain Training
Your brain is amazingly interconnected, containing around 500 trillion connections between the 100 billion brain cells in your head. It learns by spotting patterns in the world around it, whether those patterns are the rules of arithmetic or an understanding of how a flat view of a map translates into turning left or right at the next junction. Sometimes it's obvious how a certain activity will benefit your brain – for example, improving your mental arithmetic has a range of direct

benefits – but often these learned patterns are useful not just in their original context but in a wider one. It's this generalized improvement that brain training is intended to achieve.

There is a range of claims about how powerful brain training is, but it is widely accepted that the general learning effect does exist at some level. The benefit you will personally gain may well depend upon how well you exercise your brain already – if you spend all day in an unchallenging job then you stand to gain far more than someone who tackles international crises every day, for example. But even for the mentally super-fit, there are sure to be tasks in this book that will push you outside your comfort zone.

Just a few minutes of brain training every couple of days can lead to significant mental improvement, lasting not just during the period of training but for years afterwards.

The Brain Workouts
Each right-hand page in this book contains a self-contained brain workout, designed to get you thinking in ways you might not regularly try. The book is designed to be worked through in order from the front to the back, so the workouts start off relatively easy and get harder as the book progresses. They're also mixed up to ensure plenty of variety as you go. Depending upon your background and experience you're sure to find that some types are much trickier than others, but don't skip the ones you find difficult – such as the visualization or memory ones, perhaps – because these are likely to be the ones from which you will obtain most mental benefit.

Once you finish a workout then you can turn the page and check out the solution on the reverse side. If you've got a different answer then try going back and working out why this is – challenge yourself in every way you can. But don't spend a long time stuck on a task – if you can't do it in a reasonable time then come back to it later. Your brain goes on thinking without conscious effort, which is why you can return to something you have been stuck on and make sudden progress: the brain really is amazing!

Further Brain Workouts
In modern society we avoid using our memory, using phones and other devices to hold numbers, addresses, diaries, birthdays and more. Spend time deliberately practising use of your memory. Try memorizing your shopping list rather than writing it down, or challenge yourself to recall what you did throughout the day yesterday. In ancient Greece use of memory was taught as a core skill, and in many ways it is just as fundamental today. You can learn to improve it. Life is much less frustrating when you remember the things you mean to remember, and don't lose track of what you're thinking about halfway through a thought! The memory workouts in this book are just the beginning.

Seek out puzzles in newspapers, magazines and other books, or find them online on sites such as www.PuzzleMix.com. Fit them into a coffee break or try them during lunch, or whenever you can find the time. Your brain will thank you for it! Read as widely as you can. The broader your vocabulary then the more compactly you will be able to express thoughts, and the more you can hold in your memory at once while you think. Try learning foreign languages – new concepts, representations and ways of looking at the world will all benefit your brain.

Dr Gareth Moore (www.DrGarethMoore.com)

Which of these words is the odd one out, and why?

Iron	Black-out	Safety
Net	Cloak	Shower

What number comes next in this mathematical sequence?

2   3   5   8   12   17   _____

If I was born on May 1st 1953 and will be 76 years old 6 months from today, what year is it now?   _____

If the time is 8:10pm in China then it is 12:10pm in Britain, since Britain is 8 hours behind China. If it is the following times in Britain, what time is it in China?

3:25pm	4:20am	9:15pm
_____	_____	_____

If I draw 2 cards at random from a normal pack of 52 playing cards, what is the chance that I draw 2 of the same suit?   _____

How many days of the week contain the letter 'S'?   _____

Look at the following list of months and spend up to one minute trying to memorize all 8 words. Then turn the page and recall as many as possible.

February	August	October	May
March	April	November	June

Which of these words is the odd one out, and why?
Cloak – all of the rest are types of curtain.

What number comes next in this mathematical sequence?
23 – at each stage the difference increases by 1.

If I was born on May 1st 1953 and will be 76 years old 6 months from today, what year is it now?
2028.

If it's 8:10pm in China then it is 12:10pm in Britain, since Britain is 8 hours behind China. If it is the following times in Britain, what time is it in China?

3:25pm	4:20am	9:15pm
11:25pm	**12:20pm**	**5:15am**

If I draw 2 cards at random from a normal pack of 52 playing cards, what is the chance that I draw 2 of the same suit?
12 in 51 – it doesn't matter what the first card is and then there are 12 left out of the remaining 51 cards that are the same suit.

How many days of the week contain the letter 'S'?
5 days.

Recall the months:

By drawing along the existing lines, can you divide this shape up into 4 identical jigsaw pieces, with no pieces left over? The pieces may be rotated versions of one another, but you cannot mirror or 'turn over' any of the pieces.

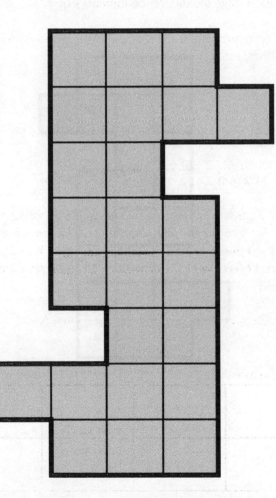

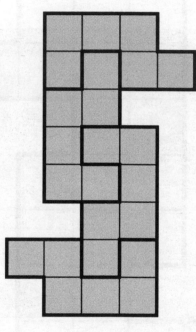

How many bricks can you count in the 3-dimensional arrangement below? Each brick is a perfect cube and the arrangement was created by starting with a 5 by 4 by 4 cuboid of bricks and then removing some bricks. You should assume that all hidden bricks – those obscured by other bricks – are still present.

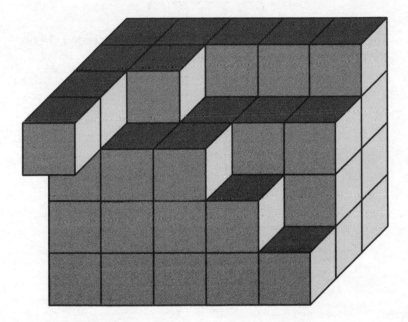

There are 51 cubes: 9 on the top level, 13 on the second, 14 on the third and 15 on the bottom level.

BRAIN CHAINS

How quickly can you solve each of the following brain chains? Without making any written notes, start with the number on the left and follow the arrows while applying each operation in turn. Write the result in the empty box at the end.

| 29 | Add forty-five | -20 | 1/2 of this | +7 | RESULT |

| 13 | +12 | ÷5 | +1 | Divide by three | RESULT |

| 17 | +19 | Square root of this | Multiply by nine | -50% | RESULT |

| 17 | -5 | 25% of this | ×11 | One third of this | RESULT |

| 39 | +15 | 50% of this | -16 | +37 | RESULT |

The results are: 34
                    2
                   27
                   11
                   48

Study the triangles below for no more than 30 seconds, then cover them over and answer the questions beneath.

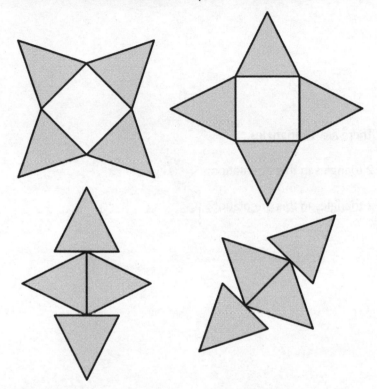

How many triangles are there?

And how many of them are in this orientation: ?

And how many in this orientation: ?

There are 16 triangles.

2 triangles in this orientation:

2 triangles in this orientation:

The same picture is shown here twice, but in each case different parts of it have been hidden behind pale grey tiles. By imagining combining the two images in your head, can you answer the following questions?

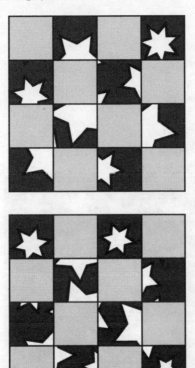

How many stars can you count in this image?

Of those stars, how many are 5-pointed?

And how many have 7 points?

11 stars.

6 5-pointed stars.

1 7-pointed star.

The combined image looks like this:

For each of the following totals, choose just 1 number from each ring of this dartboard so that those 3 numbers add up to the given total. For example, you would form a total of 10 by picking 4 from the outermost ring, 3 from the middle ring and 3 from the innermost ring.

14

26

29

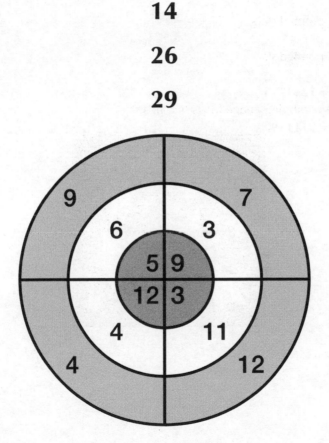

14 = 7+4+3

26 = 12+11+3

29 = 9+11+9

Mentally rearrange the 6 square tiles below in order to reveal a hidden letter or number. Keep the same overall layout of tiles (2 wide by 3 tall), and don't rotate or mirror any of the tiles.

What is revealed?

A letter 'S' is revealed.

Word Order

Look at the following list of types of grass for up to one minute. On the next page you will find the same list of words but in a different order. When time is up, turn the page and see how accurately you can recall the original position of each of the words.

Bamboo	Oat	Maize
Rice	Rye	Millet
Wheat	Barley	Reed

Missing Words

Once you have completed the above task, try this one too. Study these two lists of related words for one minute, then turn the page and try to spot which word is missing from each list.

dog   cat   gerbil
    hamster   fish

green   orange   yellow
    red   blue

Word Order

Try to place the grasses back in their original boxes:

Millet	Oat	Rice
Rye	Wheat	Bamboo
Maize	Reed	Barley

Now turn back to the previous page for the second task.

Missing Words

Can you spot which word is missing from each list?

gerbil	dog	_____
cat	hamster	

yellow	green	_____
red	blue	

Now turn back to check your answer.

COMPREHENSION

*Read the following passage and then answer the questions below **without** referring back to the text. Once you have answered as many questions as you can, read the text a second time and see if you can then answer all the remaining questions.*

As the first stray fingers of sunlight searched out the gaps in the curtains, Rachel's alarm clock awoke with the merry tune of holiday. She grumbled awake only to be arrested with a sudden spark of pleasure, for today was the first day of freedom: no more 8am starts and no more office politics; no more incompetent managers and no more arrogant colleagues. This was the beginning; a new dawn both real and metaphorical.

She leapt out of bed with uncharacteristic vigour, skipping her usual breakfast cereal in her excitement to get to the airport and all that it entailed. Soon she was checked in and waiting at the gate, and before long she was on her way to Rome.

What time did Rachel usually start the day at?

Who is described as 'arrogant'?

What is described as having 'fingers'?

What was her opinion of her managers?

Name three unusual things about her morning routine today, prior to her departure for the airport.

What time did Rachel usually start the day at?
8am.

Who is described as 'arrogant'?
Her colleagues.

What is described as having 'fingers'?
Sunlight.

What was her opinion of her managers?
They were incompetent.

*Name three unusual things about her morning routine today,
prior to her departure for the airport.*
**She is on holiday and doesn't have to go to work. She also
skipped her breakfast cereal, and leapt out of bed with
uncharacteristic vigour.**

Spend no more than one minute studying the top picture.
When time is up, cover it over and redraw it as accurately as
you can on the empty grid below.

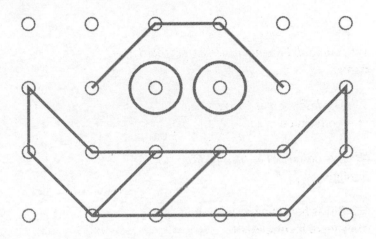

Now try to redraw the same image on this blank page. You can turn back and study it for as long as you like before attempting this task.

Given the following set of numbers and mathematical signs, can you rearrange them to obtain the given result?

You must use all of the numbers and signs, but you can use as many additional 'brackets' as you like.

For example, (4×3) − (2×5) = 2.

1	3	4	5	7
+	+	×	÷	

RESULT: 6

Now try to do the same with this set too:

1	2	3	4	5
+	+	×	÷	

RESULT: 25

$$(((7 \times 3) + 4) \div 5) + 1 = \mathbf{6}$$

$$(((1 + 2) \div 3) + 4) \times 5 = \mathbf{25}$$

Draw solid lines along some of the dashed lines in order to divide the grid up into a set of rectangles, so that every number is inside only one rectangle. The number inside each rectangle must be exactly equal to the number of grid squares that the rectangle contains.

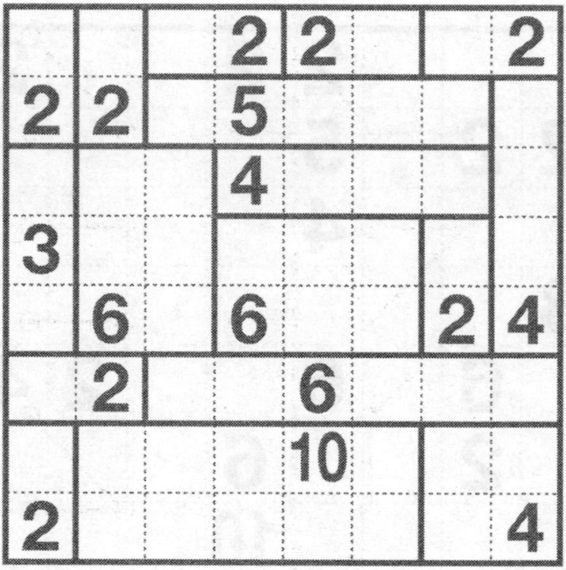
2 2 2
2 2 5
4
3
6 6 2 4
2 6
10
2 4

Imagine placing a two-sided mirror on the dashed vertical line.
Can you draw what you would see reflected on each side of the
mirror?

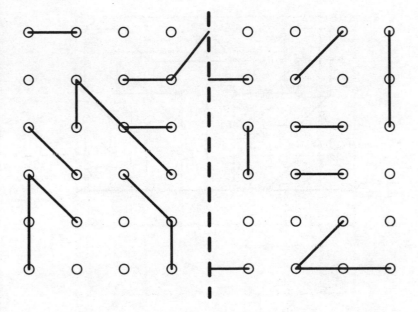

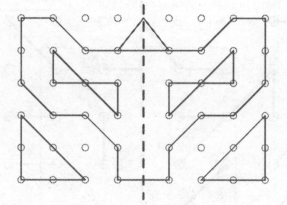

SHAPE LINK

In each of the following two puzzles, can you connect each pair of identical shapes together by drawing only horizontal and vertical lines from square to square? No more than one line can enter each square, which means that the lines can't touch or cross. The example solution on the right should help clarify the rules.

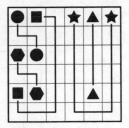

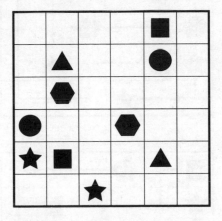

39

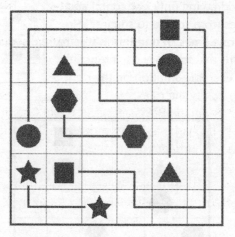

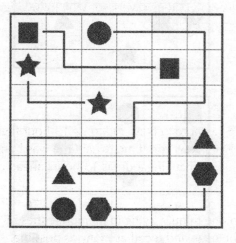

Which of these words is the odd one out, and why?

Currant   **Fig**   **Prune**   **Sultana**   **Raisin**

What number comes next in this mathematical sequence?

729   243   81   27   9   3   _____

The sum of Adrian and Bob's ages is 8, while Charlie is twice as old as Adrian. If Charlie is 1 year older than Bob, then how old is each of the 3 children?

_____

Today I drove to the shops at an average of 42mph (miles per hour) and got there in 30 minutes. How far away is my work?

_____

I have removed all of the vowels from the following words. What were they originally?

PLMG   **TRNST**   **NTQ**

_____   _____   _____

If I fly from Singapore to New York on a 19-hour flight and arrive at 1:00pm New York time, what time was it in Singapore when I left, given that Singapore is 13 hours ahead of New York?

_____

Spend up to one minute trying to memorize these 8 words. Then turn the page and recall as many as possible.

Prime	**Integer**	**Complex**	**Real**
Irrational	**Perfect**	**Fractional**	**Whole**

Which of these words is the odd one out, and why?
Fig – all of the rest are always dried fruit.

What number comes next in this mathematical sequence?
1 – each number is the previous one divided by 3.

The sum of Adrian and Bob's ages is 8, while Charlie is twice as old as Adrian. If Charlie is 1 year older than Bob, then how old is each of the three children?
Adrian is 3, Bob is 5 and Charlie is 6.

Today I drove to the shops at an average of 42mph (miles per hour) and got there in 30 minutes. How far away is my work?
21 miles away.

I have removed all of the vowels from the following words. What were they originally?
PLUMAGE   TRANSIT   ANTIQUE

If I fly from Singapore to New York on a 19-hour flight and arrive at 1:00pm New York time, what time was it in Singapore when I left, given that Singapore is 13 hours ahead of New York?
7:00am. If I arrive at 1:00pm NY time then I set out at 6:00pm NY time, which is 7:00am Singapore time.

Recall the types of number:

The same picture is shown here twice, but in each case different parts of it have been hidden behind pale grey tiles. By imagining combining the two images in your head, can you answer the following questions?

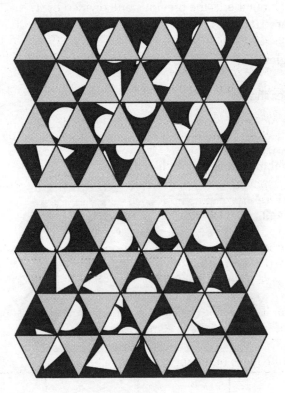

How many white circles are there?

And how many white triangles can you count?

Are there any other white shapes present?

There are 10 circles.

8 triangles.

No other shapes.

The combined image looks like this:

Study the stars below for no more than 30 seconds, then cover them over and answer the questions beneath.

How many stars are there in total?

How many stars are there in the largest pile of grey stars?

How many stars overlap with the white star in the centre?

13 stars in total.

The largest pile has 4 stars.

The white star overlaps with 3 stars.

JIGSAW CUT

By drawing along the existing lines, can you divide this shape up into 4 identical jigsaw pieces, with no pieces left over? The pieces may be rotated versions of one another, but you cannot mirror or 'turn over' any of the pieces.

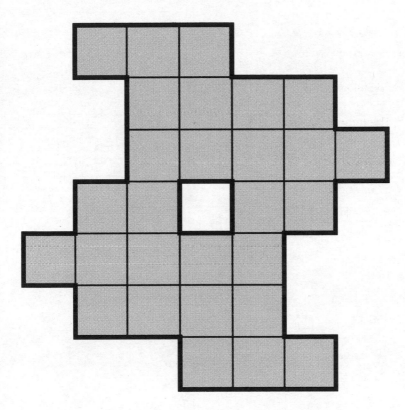

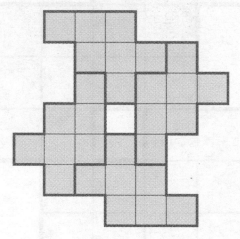

EQUATION FINDER

Given the following set of numbers and mathematical signs, can you rearrange them to obtain the given result?

You must use all of the numbers and signs, but you can use as many additional 'brackets' as you like.

For example, (4×3) − (2×5) = 2.

2	3	3	4	10
+	×	×	÷	

RESULT: 51

Now try to do the same with this set too:

2	3	5	7	25
+	−	×	×	

RESULT: 124

$(4 + (10 \times 3)) \div 2 \times 3 = \mathbf{51}$

$(25 - 3) \times 5 + (2 \times 7) = \mathbf{124}$

Mentally rearrange the six square tiles below in order to reveal a hidden letter or number. Don't rotate or mirror any of the tiles.

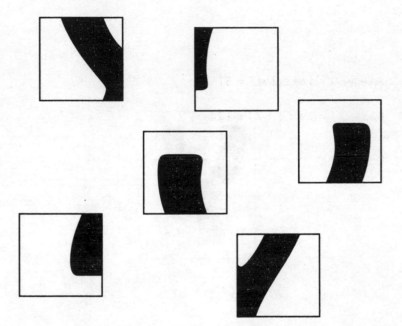

What is revealed?

A letter 'Y' is revealed.

For each of the following totals, choose just 1 number from
each ring of this dartboard so that those 4 numbers add up to
the given total. For example, you would form a total of 9 by
picking 3, 3, 2 and 1 from the outer- to the innermost rings
respectively.

11

20

34

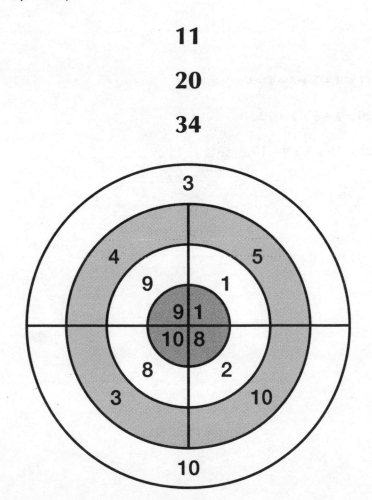

11 = 3 + 5 + 2 + 1

20 = 3 + 5 + 2 + 10

34 = 10 + 5 + 9 + 10

BRAIN CHAINS

How quickly can you solve each of the following brain chains?
Without making any written notes, start with the number on
the left and follow the arrows while applying each operation in
turn. Write the result in the empty box at the end.

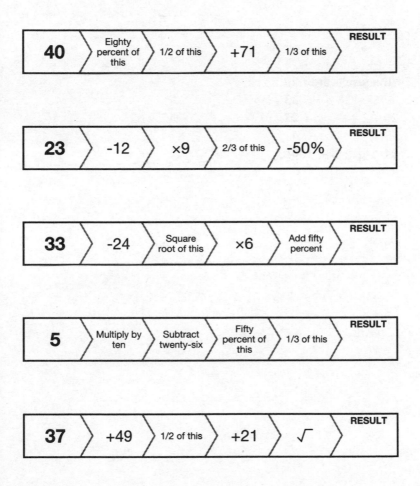

| 40 | Eighty percent of this | 1/2 of this | +71 | 1/3 of this | RESULT |

| 23 | -12 | ×9 | 2/3 of this | -50% | RESULT |

| 33 | -24 | Square root of this | ×6 | Add fifty percent | RESULT |

| 5 | Multiply by ten | Subtract twenty-six | Fifty percent of this | 1/3 of this | RESULT |

| 37 | +49 | 1/2 of this | +21 | √ | RESULT |

The results are: 29
33
27
4
8

Can you connect each pair of identical
shapes together by drawing only
horizontal and vertical lines from square
to square? No more than one line can
enter each square, which means that the
lines can't touch or cross. The example
solution on the right should help clarify
the rules.

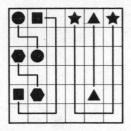

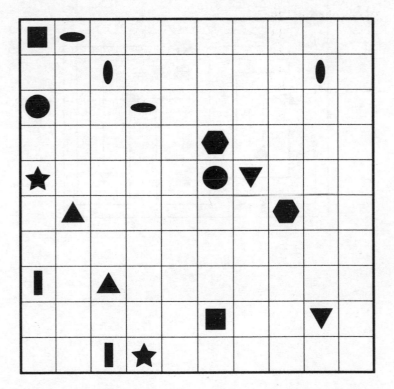

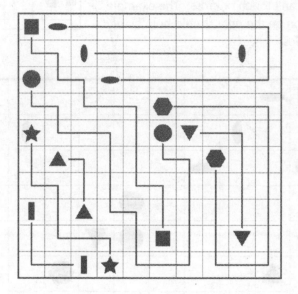

Spend no more than one minute studying the top picture. When time is up, cover it over and redraw it as accurately as you can on the empty grid below.

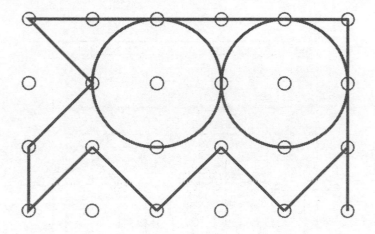

Now try to redraw the same image on this blank page. You can turn back and study it for as long as you like before attempting this task.

*Read the following passage and then answer the questions below **without** referring back to the text. Once you have answered as many questions as you can, read the text a second time and see if you can then answer all the remaining questions.*

Four dog walkers are out for a Sunday afternoon stroll in Penylan Park, when a sudden downpour forces them into the old black-and-white Victorian park pavilion. Most of the benches are covered in the excess of the roof's many pigeons, but they manage to find one clean bench. All four sit down on the bench in a row, facing the same direction.

Jane is sitting further left on the bench than Dave, who is not at the very end. Penny is in one of the two middle positions, but neither of her immediate neighbours is Ian. Each of the four people has their dog on a lead, and each dog is sitting directly in front of its owner. Every dog shares the initial letter of its name with its owner.

What colour is the pavilion they are sitting in?

Is the pavilion closer to 10, 50 or 150 years old?

Who is sitting furthest to the right on the bench?

The four dogs are named Dogmo, Incher, Jubbalo and Pango. Which two of these four dogs are sitting between other dogs?

What is the name of the park they are all in?

Why did they all have to sit on the same bench?

What colour is the pavilion they are sitting in?
Black-and-white.

Is the pavilion closer to 10, 50 or 150 years old?
150 years old, since it dates from the Victorian era.

Who is sitting furthest to the right on the bench?
Ian. (The full order, left to right, is Jane, Penny, Dave, Ian).

The four dogs are named Dogmo, Incher, Jubbalo and Pango.
Which two of these four dogs are sitting between other dogs?
Pango and **Dogmo**, given that each dog is sitting in front of its owner.

What is the name of the park they are all in?
Penylan Park.

Why did they all have to sit on the same bench?
Because the pigeons had made a mess of all the other benches.

Can you redraw the top picture on the bottom grid while rotating it a quarter turn (90 degrees) clockwise, as indicated by the arrow? Try to do this without rotating the book at all!

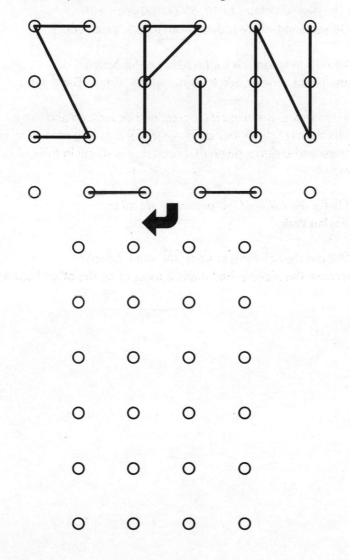

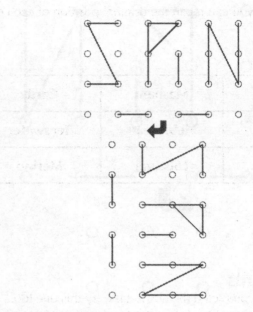

Word Order

Look at the following list of breeds of sheep for up to one minute. On the next page you will find the same list of words but in a different order. When time is up, turn the page and see how accurately you can recall the original position of each of the words.

Shetland	Masham	Cardy
Lonk	Hebridean	Teeswater
Portland	Lacaune	Merino

Missing Words

Once you have completed the above task, try this one too. Study these two lists of related words for one minute, then turn the page and try to spot which word is missing from each list.

tulip   dandelion   poppy
rose   daisy

marmalade   jam   conserve
jelly   purée

WORD MEMORY

Word Order

Try to place the sheep back in their original boxes:

Teeswater	Portland	Merino
Cardy	Lonk	Hebridean
Shetland	Masham	Lacaune

Now turn back to the previous page for the second task.

Missing Words

Can you spot which word is missing from each list?

poppy   rose   _____
    dandelion   tulip

jam   purée   _____
    jelly   marmalade

Now turn back to check your answer.

Draw solid lines along some of the dashed lines in order to divide the grid up into a set of rectangles, so that every number is inside only one rectangle. The number inside each rectangle must be exactly equal to the number of grid squares that the rectangle contains.

			4				**2**
			9				
				8			
3						**7**	
		4					
8							**4**
			2		**6**		
		5					**2**

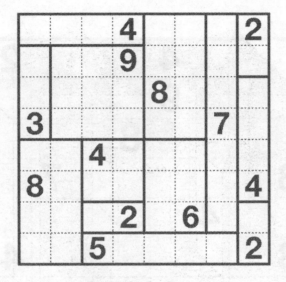

In the 3-dimensional arrangement below, how many cube bricks are there in total in columns capped with pyramid bricks? Assume that any hidden cube bricks – those obscured by other bricks – are present and that the structure is no more than 4 cube bricks plus 1 pyramid brick tall at any point.

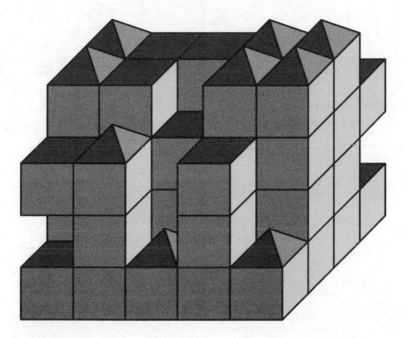

And how many cube bricks are there in the arrangement in total? The arrangement was created by starting with a 5 by 4 by 4 cuboid of bricks and then removing some bricks. Then once complete pyramid shapes were added on top of some columns of bricks – do not count these. You should assume that all hidden cube bricks are still present.

There are 29 cubes in total directly beneath the pyramid caps.

There are 63 cubes – by level from the top down there are 9, 18, 16 and 20 respectively.

Which of these words is the odd one out, and why?

Curling	Skiing	Skeleton
Luge	Toboggan	Bobsled

What number comes next in this mathematical sequence?

1   4   9   16   25   36   _____

If I roll two ordinary 6-sided dice, what is the likelihood that I end up with a total of 11?

_____

If my cat has 7 kittens, each of which has 5 kittens of its own, and then each of those has another 3 kittens, how many kittens are there in that final generation of kittens?

_____

A half-mile-long train enters a tunnel at 30 miles per hour. If the tunnel is 2 miles in length, for how long is any part of the train in the tunnel?

_____

What is the maximum number of Tuesdays in any calendar year?

_____

What were these three words before I removed all the vowels?

NVRSL _____   RBBTD _____   RDVRK _____

Spend up to one minute trying to memorize these 8 desserts. Then turn the page and recall as many as possible.

Ice cream	Strudel	Cheesecake	Pie
Trifle	Crumble	Profiterole	Jelly

Which of these words is the odd one out, and why?
Curling – all are winter sports but the rest involve riding on skis or a sled of some description.

What number comes next in this mathematical sequence?
49 – these are the squares of 1, 2, 3 etc, or alternatively the difference increases by 2 at each step.

If I roll two ordinary 6-sided dice, what is the likelihood that I end up with a total of 11?
2 in 36 (or 1 in 18), since there are 2 possible ways of getting 11 (5+6, 6+5) out of the 36 (6×6) possible combinations of the two dice.

If my cat has 7 kittens, each of which has 5 kittens of its own, and then each of those has another 3 kittens, how many kittens are there in that final generation of kittens?
105 kittens, or 7 × 5 × 3.

A half-mile-long train enters a tunnel at 30 miles per hour. If the tunnel is 2 miles in length, for how long is any part of the train in the tunnel?
5 minutes.

What is the maximum number of Tuesdays in any calendar year?
53 Tuesdays.

What were these three words before I removed all the vowels?
UNIVERSAL   RABBITED   AARDVARK

Recall the desserts:

For each of the following totals, choose just 1 number from
each ring of this dartboard so that those 3 numbers add up to
the given total. For example, you would form a total of 15 by
picking 5 from the outermost ring, 3 from the middle ring and 7
from the innermost ring.

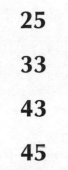

25

33

43

45

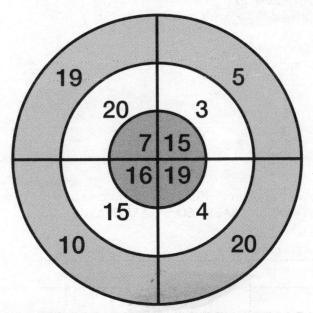

25 = 5 + 4 + 16

33 = 10 + 4 + 19

43 = 20 + 4 + 19

45 = 10 + 20 + 15

BRAIN CHAINS

How quickly can you solve each of the following brain chains?
Without making any written notes, start with the number on
the left and follow the arrows while applying each operation in
turn. Write the result in the empty box at the end.

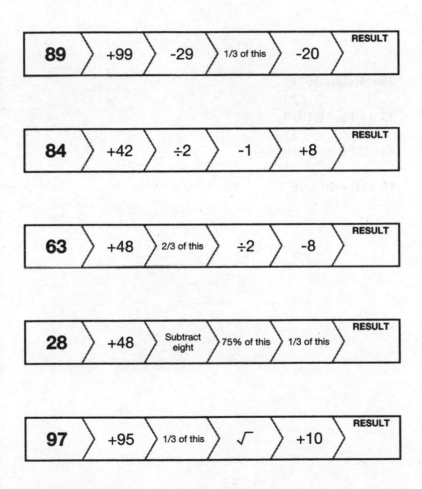

| 89 | +99 | -29 | 1/3 of this | -20 | **RESULT** |

| 84 | +42 | ÷2 | -1 | +8 | **RESULT** |

| 63 | +48 | 2/3 of this | ÷2 | -8 | **RESULT** |

| 28 | +48 | Subtract eight | 75% of this | 1/3 of this | **RESULT** |

| 97 | +95 | 1/3 of this | √ | +10 | **RESULT** |

BRAIN CHAINS

The results are: 33
                   70
                   29
                   17
                   18

By drawing along the existing lines, can you divide this shape up into 4 identical jigsaw pieces, with no pieces left over? The pieces may be rotated versions of one another, but you cannot mirror or 'turn over' any of the pieces.

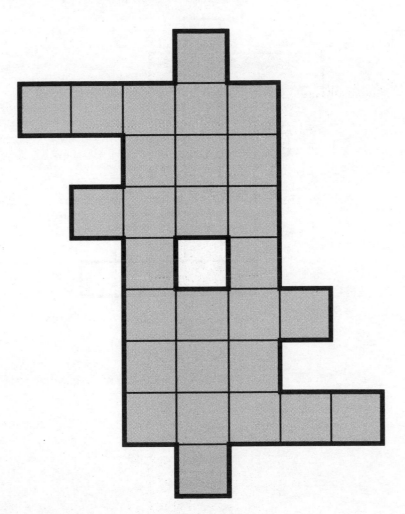

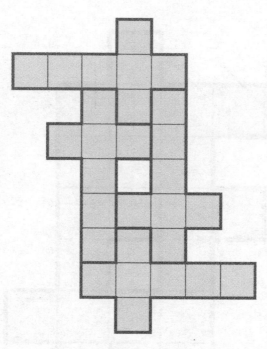

REFLECT ON THIS

Imagine placing a two-sided mirror on the dashed vertical line. Can you draw what you would see reflected on each side of the mirror?

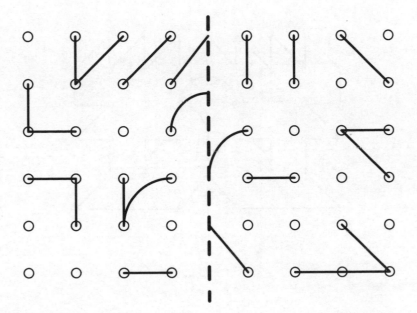

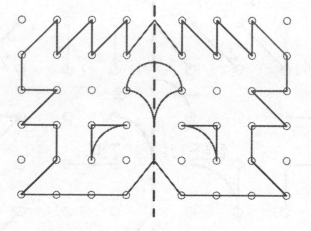

Given the following set of numbers and mathematical signs, can you rearrange them to obtain the given result?

You must use all of the numbers and signs, but you can use as many additional 'brackets' as you like.

For example, $(4 \times 3) - (2 \times 5) = 2$.

7	7	7	7	7
+	+	×	×	

RESULT: 735

Now try to do the same with this set too:

1	6	11	16	61
+	−	−	×	

RESULT: 47

$$((7 + 7) \times 7 + 7) \times 7) = \mathbf{735}$$

$$(16 \times 6) + 1 - (61 - 11) = \mathbf{47}$$

Can you connect each pair of identical shapes together by drawing only horizontal and vertical lines from square to square? No more than one line can enter each square, which means that the lines can't touch or cross. The example solution on the right should help clarify the rules.

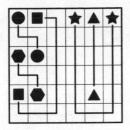

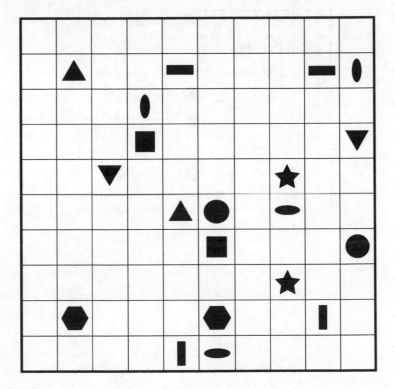

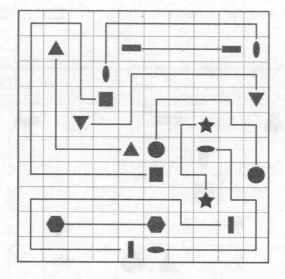

Study the picture below of partially transparent circles and ellipses for no more than 30 seconds, then cover it over and answer the questions beneath.

How many ellipses (excluding circles) are there?

What is the greatest number of circles overlapping at any point in the picture?

How many circles are overlapped by an ellipse?

And at how many different orientations are ellipses shown?

There are 8 ellipses (excluding circles).

The greatest number of overlapping circles is 3.

6 circles are overlapped by an ellipse.

There are 4 orientations of ellipse.

*Read the following passage and then answer the questions below **without** referring back to the text. Once you have answered as many questions as you can, read the text a second time and see if you can then answer all the remaining questions.*

If I could leap forward in time, would I choose to? If I jumped a hundred years into the future what would I see? One day it might be possible to do exactly this, thanks to the phenomenon of time dilation described by Einstein's theories of relativity: the faster you travel through space so the faster you move forward in time. If you fly from the UK to the US you jump forward several billionths of a second in time – not much, but it can be measured.

Research into viable cryogenic suspension might also one day permit us to be held in stasis for arbitrary periods of time without ageing. If you could go into a chamber and then come back out in the future, would you? Your friends and family would be older, or gone, and who knows what kind of world you might awaken to? We might have discovered the secret of gravity, so the world could be full of flying cars. Or we may have simulated the human brain, and created computers far more intelligent than any of us. Would there be humanoid robots everywhere, and would we be officially redundant?

What sort of artificial suspension is being researched?
What is the name of the time phenomenon I refer to?
What is my first worry about the future that I mention?
How far forward in time do you travel if you fly from the UK to the US?
How many years into the future do I suggest travelling?
What might we simulate in the future?

What sort of artificial suspension is being researched?
Cryogenic suspension.

What is the name of the time phenomenon I refer to?
Time dilation.

What is my first worry about the future that I mention?
Friends and family being older or gone.

How far forward in time do you travel if you fly from the UK to the US?
Several billionths of a second.

How many years into the future do I suggest travelling?
A hundred years.

What might we simulate in the future?
The human brain.

Mentally rearrange the 6 square tiles below in order to reveal a hidden letter, number or symbol. Keep the same overall layout of tiles (2 wide by 3 tall), and don't rotate or mirror any of the tiles.

What is revealed?

A dollar sign '$' is revealed.

Word Order

Look at the following list of island groups for up to one minute. On the next page you will find the same list of words but in a different order. When time is up, turn the page and see how accurately you can recall the original position of each of the groups.

Faeroes	Grenadines	Aegean
British Virgin	Canaries	Loyalty
Falkland	Leeward	Philippines
Marshall	Windward	Tuvalu

Missing Words

Once you have completed the above task, try this one too. Study these two lists of related words for one minute, then turn the page and try to spot which word is missing from each list.

tracing	copying	printing
reproducing	faxing	duplicating

transitory	passing	fleeting
brief	short	temporary

Word Order

Try to place the island groups back in their original boxes:

Loyalty	Windward	Marshall
Tuvalu	Philippines	Aegean
Falkland	British Virgin	Canaries
Grenadines	Leeward	Faeroes

Now turn back to the previous page for the second task.

Missing Words

Can you spot which word is missing from each list?

faxing	duplicating	copying
printing	reproducing	_____

temporary	short	transitory
passing	brief	_____

Now turn back to check your answer.

The same picture is shown here twice, but in each case different parts of it have been hidden behind pale grey tiles. By imagining combining the two images in your head, can you answer the following questions?

There are three chains of identically orientated triangles here – how many triangles are in the longest chain?

And how many triangles can you count in total?

How many circles are there?

The longest chain has 5 triangles.

13 triangles in total.

17 circles.

The combined image looks like this:

Draw solid lines along some of the dashed lines in order to divide the grid up into a set of rectangles, so that every number is inside only one rectangle. The number inside each rectangle must be exactly equal to the number of grid squares that the rectangle contains.

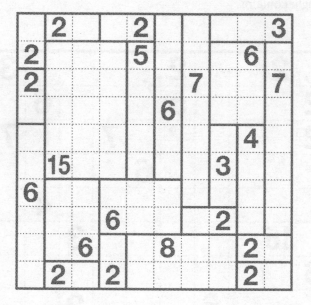

Spend no more than one minute studying the top picture.
When time is up, cover it over and redraw it as accurately as
you can on the empty grid below.

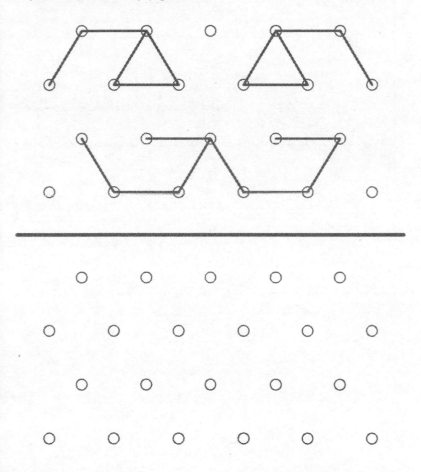

Now try to redraw the same image on this blank page. You can turn back and study it for as long as you like before attempting this task.

How many bricks can you count in the 3-dimensional arrangement below? Each brick is a perfect cube and the arrangement was created by starting with a 5 by 4 by 4 cuboid of bricks and then removing some bricks. You should assume that all hidden bricks – those obscured by other bricks – are still present.

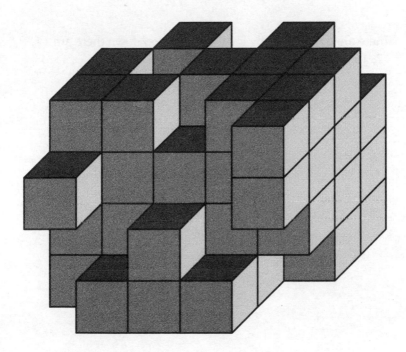

There are 61 cubes – by level from the top down there are 11, 17, 16 and 17 respectively.

Which of these words is the odd one out, and why?

Hood	Proof	More
Less	Minder	Care

What number comes next in this mathematical sequence?

4   6   10   16   26   42   _____

If I take 2 socks at random from a drawer containing 2 red socks, 3 blue socks and 5 green socks, what is the chance that I pull out a matching pair?   _____

I draw 4 shapes in a row in my notepad. The square is next to the circle, while the circle is further right than the star. There is 1 shape between the star and the square, and the triangle is further right than the circle. In what order have I drawn the shapes?

_____

If I add up the first 8 prime numbers, from 2 to 19 inclusive, what is the result?   _____

I have removed all of the vowels from the following words. What were they originally?

LFY	TMNL	XTD
_____	_____	_____

Spend up to one minute trying to memorize these 8 words. Then turn the page and recall as many as possible.

Jog	Tear	Race	Hurry
Speed	Rush	Dart	Run

MIXED PUZZLES

Which of these words is the odd one out, and why?
More – all of the rest can be prefixed by 'child'.

What number comes next in this mathematical sequence?
68 – each number is the sum of the previous two.

If I take 2 socks at random from a drawer containing 2 red socks, 3 blue socks and 5 green socks, what is the chance that I pull out a matching pair?
28 in 90 (or 14 in 45). There is a 2/10 chance of picking a red sock first with a 1/9 chance of the second sock also being red, so the likelihood of a red pair is 2/10 × 1/9 = 2/90. Then similarly the likelihoods of a blue pair is 6/90 and a green pair is 20/90. Add these possible options to give 28/90.

I draw 4 shapes in a row in my notepad. The square is next to the circle, while the circle is further right than the star. There is 1 shape between the star and the square, and the triangle is further right than the circle. In what order have I drawn the shapes?
From left to right: star, circle, square, triangle.

If I add up the first 8 prime numbers, from 2 to 19 inclusive, what is the result?
77. In other words, 2+3+5+7+11+13+17+19.

I have removed all of the vowels from the following words. What were they originally?
LEAFY   AUTUMNAL   EXITED

Recall the words:

By drawing along the existing lines, can you divide this shape up into 4 identical jigsaw pieces, with no pieces left over? The pieces may be rotated versions of one another, but you cannot mirror or 'turn over' any of the pieces.

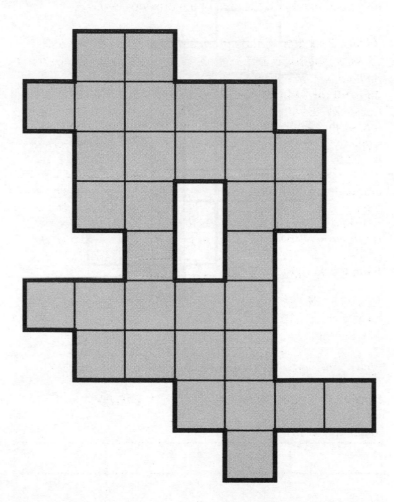

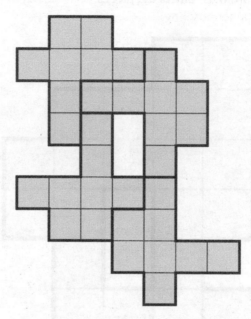

For each of the following totals, choose just 1 number from each ring of this dartboard so that those 3 numbers add up to the given total. For example, you would form a total of 23 by picking 12 from the outermost ring, 6 from the middle ring and 5 from the innermost ring.

30

37

45

52

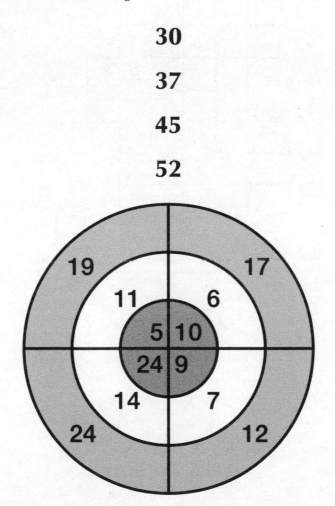

30 = 19 + 6 + 5

37 = 17 + 11 + 9

45 = 24 + 11 + 10

52 = 17 + 11 + 24

Spend no more than one minute studying the top picture. When time is up, cover it over and redraw it as accurately as you can on the empty grid below.

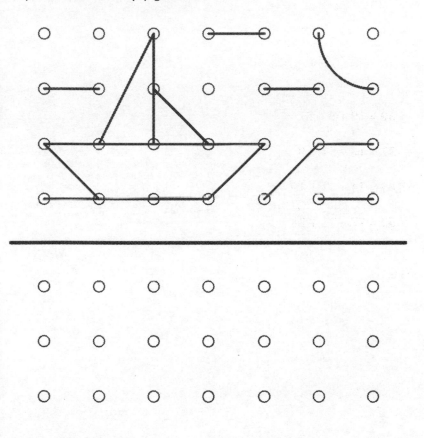

Now try to redraw the same image on this blank page. You can turn back and study it for as long as you like before attempting this task.

*Read the following passage and then answer the questions below **without** referring back to the text. Once you have answered as many questions as you can, read the text a second time and see if you can then answer all the remaining questions.*

If you name your child after a flower, or a season, or a place, or a virtue, at some point the inevitable gods of irony will strike. What if Joy is unhappy, or Faith loses hers? Chastity might lose her way, and Hope feel depressed. Liberty could turn out to be a tyrant, or join with Justice to break the law.

Spring might well bounce through life, but is Autumn destined for a fall? A Rose may blossom, but Daisy could spend her life in chains. River might work in current affairs, but Sunday could choose not to work at all. Ruby might shine, but Pearl may simply clam up.

Best to play it safe. Don't heteronym-name

Who is it suggested might one day be unhappy?

What might happen to Justice?

Who is it said might strike if you name your child after a flower, season, place or virtue?

Who is seemingly destined for a fall?

What job is mentioned as particularly apt for River?

What is it said not to do in the final sentence?

Who is it suggested might one day be unhappy?
Joy.

What might happen to Justice?
He might break the law.

Who is it said might strike if you name your child after a flower, season, place or virtue?
The gods of irony.

Who is seemingly destined for a fall?
Autumn.

What job is mentioned as particularly apt for River?
Current affairs.

What is it said not to do in the final sentence?
Heteronym-name.

CUBIC COUNTING INTERMEDIATE

How many bricks can you count in the 3-dimensional
arrangement below? Each brick is a perfect cube and the
arrangement was created by starting with a 5 by 4 by 8 cuboid
of bricks and then removing some bricks. You should assume
that all hidden bricks – those obscured by other bricks – are still
present.

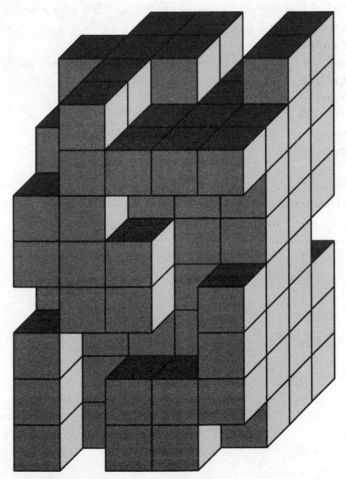

There are 134 cubes – by level from the top down there are 9, 19, 17, 18, 17, 17, 19 and 18 respectively.

Mentally join together the six square tiles below in order to reveal a hidden letter or number. You will need to rotate some or all of the tiles, but do not mirror (or 'flip over') any of them.

What is revealed?

A letter 'X' is revealed.

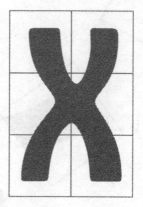

Given the following set of numbers and mathematical signs, can you rearrange them to obtain the given result?

You must use all of the numbers and signs, but you can use as many additional 'brackets' as you like.

For example, (4×3) − (2×5) = 2.

$$2 \qquad 4 \qquad 6 \qquad 8 \qquad 10$$

$$+ \qquad + \qquad \times \qquad \times$$

RESULT: 624

Now try to do the same with this set too:

$$3 \qquad 5 \qquad 7 \qquad 9 \qquad 11 \qquad 13$$

$$+ \qquad - \qquad - \qquad \times \qquad \times$$

RESULT: 664

$$(((2 + 8) \times 10) + 4) \times 6 = \textbf{624}$$

$$(((13 - 3) \times 7) + 5) \times 9 - 11 = \textbf{664}$$

Study the stars below for no more than 30 seconds, then cover them over and answer the questions beneath.

How many black stars are there?

If this star is the 'right way up': , then how many stars are upside down?

How many white stars are there in the middle column?

Is there any row or column with all stars the right way up?

3 black stars.

3 stars upside down.

No white stars in the middle column.

There are no rows or columns with all of the stars the right way up.

BRAIN CHAINS

How quickly can you solve each of the following brain chains?
Without making any written notes, start with the number on
the left and follow the arrows while applying each operation in
turn. Write the result in the empty box at the end.

| 29 | +163 | 75% of this | ÷9 | ×4 | RESULT |

| 90 | ÷6 | +78 | 2/3 of this | +126 | RESULT |

| 126 | -19 | +109 | Divide by four | +104 | RESULT |

| 57 | ÷3 | +97 | 1/4 of this | Add two | RESULT |

| 92 | 1/2 of this | ÷2 | +148 | ÷3 | RESULT |

119

The results are: 64
                  188
                  158
                  31
                  57

The same picture is shown here twice, but in the bottom image it has been rotated half a revolution (180 degrees). Also in each case different parts of it have been hidden behind pale grey tiles. By imagining combining and rotating the two images in your head, can you answer the following questions?

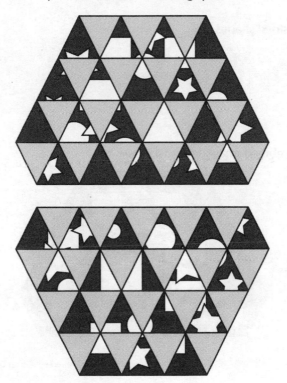

How many stars are there?

And how many four-sided shapes?

Finally, how many circles can you count?

8 stars.

5 four-sided shapes.

5 circles.

The combined image looks like this:

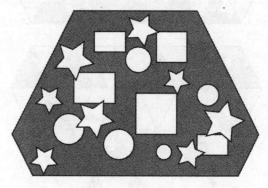

Word Order

Look at the following list of currencies for up to one minute. On the next page you will find the same list of words but in a different order. When time is up, turn the page and see how accurately you can recall the original position of each of the words.

Dollar	Baht	Peso
Yen	Yuan	Zloty
Krone	Euro	Dram
Dinar	Pound	Won

Missing Words

Once you have completed the above task, try this one too. Study these two lists of related words for one minute, then turn the page and try to spot which word is missing from each list.

achievement	success	completion
victory	attainment	fulfilment

defeat	collapse	debacle
calamity	misfortune	fiasco

WORD MEMORY

Word Order

Try to place the currencies back in their original boxes:

Pound	Won	Krone
Zloty	Dinar	Euro
Dram	Yuan	Yen
Peso	Dollar	Baht

Now turn back to the previous page for the second task.

Missing Words

Can you spot which word is missing from each list?

victory	attainment	fulfilment
completion	achievement	_____

collapse	fiasco	misfortune
defeat	debacle	_____

Now turn back to check your answer.

Draw solid lines along some of the dashed lines in order to divide the grid up into a set of rectangles, so that every number is inside only one rectangle. The number inside each rectangle must be exactly equal to the number of grid squares that the rectangle contains.

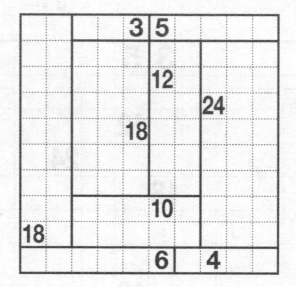

Can you connect each pair of identical shapes together by drawing only horizontal and vertical lines from square to square? No more than one line can enter each square, which means that the lines can't touch or cross. The example solution on the right should help clarify the rules.

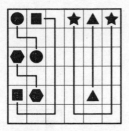

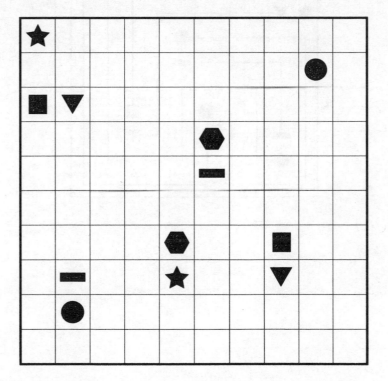

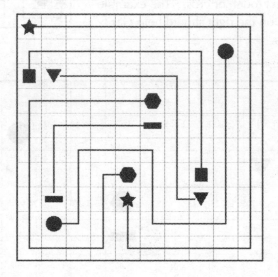

Can you redraw the top picture on the bottom grid while rotating it clockwise through half a revolution (180 degrees), as indicated by the arrow? Try to do this without rotating the book at all!

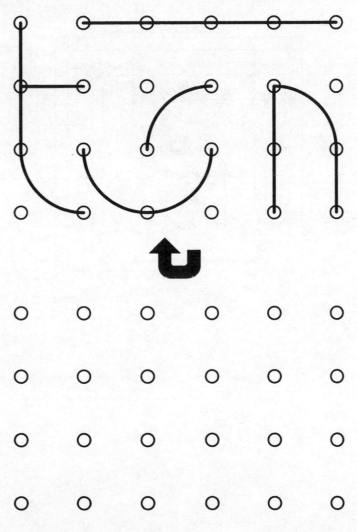

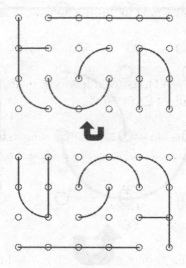

Which of these words is the odd one out, and why?

Drift	**Plough**	**Ball**
Storm	**Globe**	**Wander**

What number comes next in this mathematical sequence?

2   **5**   **11**   **23**   **47**   **95**   _____

Using a phone keypad to convert letters to digits, what is the mathematical result of CAT+DOG?   _____

Try this creative task. In each of the following industries what might these fictitious acronyms stand for? NI could be No Idea!

Fashion	**UPC**	_____
Television	**DDM**	_____
Advertising	**REP**	_____

If each day was one hour shorter, how many full extra days could be fitted into the normal-duration month of January?

_____

To convert Fahrenheit to Celsius you subtract 32, multiply by 5 and divide by 9. But if the temperature is 35 degrees Celsius, what is that in Fahrenheit?

_____

Look at the following list of people and spend up to one minute trying to memorise all nine words. Then turn the page and recall as many as possible.

Actor	**Medic**	**Miner**	**Mason**	**Farmer**
	Carpenter	**Pilot**	**Valet**	**Typist**

Which of these words is the odd one out, and why?
Wander – all of the rest can be prefixed by 'snow'.

What number comes next in this mathematical sequence?
191. At each step the difference doubles.

Using a phone keypad to convert letters to numbers, what is the mathematical result of CAT+DOG?
592. CAT+DOG = 228+364

Try this creative task. In each of the following industries what might these fictitious acronyms stand for? NI could be No Idea!
There is no fixed solution for this, but some ideas are:

> UPC   Unbelievably Pretentious Clothing.
> DDM   Don't Dare Miss.
> REP   Ridiculously Expensive Product.

If each day was one hour shorter, how many full extra days could be fitted into the normal-duration month of January?
1 day. You'd have 29 shorter days plus 8 hours remaining.

To convert Fahrenheit to Celsius you subtract 32, multiply by 5 and divide by 9. But if the temperature is 35 degrees Celsius, what is that in Fahrenheit?
95 degrees Fahrenheit.

Recall the people:

Given the following set of numbers and mathematical signs, can you rearrange them to obtain the given result?

You must use all of the numbers and signs, but you can use as many additional 'brackets' as you like.

For example, (4×3) − (2×5) = 2.

3   6   9   12   15

+   +   ×   ÷

RESULT: 5

Now try to do the same with this set too:

5   15   20   25   25

+   +   ×   ÷

RESULT: 17

$(((9+6) \times 3) + 15) \div 12 = \mathbf{5}$

$(((5+15) \times 20) + 25) \div 25 = \mathbf{17}$

The same picture is shown here twice, but in each case different parts of it have been hidden behind pale grey tiles. By imagining combining the two images in your head, can you answer the following questions?

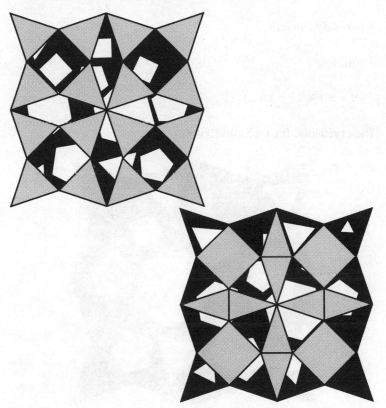

How many white triangles can you count?

How many white five-sided shapes can you find?

And how many white squares can you count?

5 triangles.

4 five-sided shapes.

3 squares.

The combined image looks like this:

MEMORY REDRAW

Spend no more than one minute studying the top picture.
When time is up, cover it over and redraw it as accurately as
you can on the empty grid below.

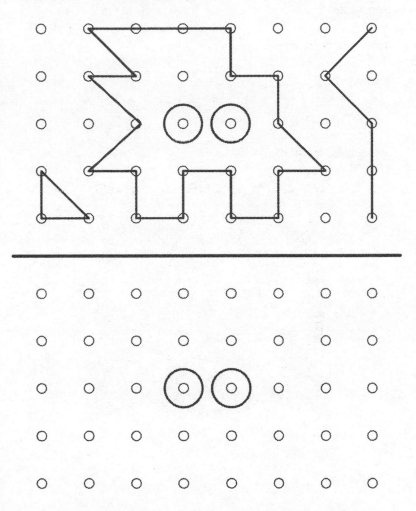

Now try to redraw the same image on this blank page. You can turn back and study it for as long as you like before attempting this task.

*Read the following poem as slowly as you like and then answer the questions below **without** referring back to the text. Once you have answered as many questions as you can, read the text a second time and see if you can then answer all the remaining questions.*

If ever love as perfect knew,
As you and I, and me and you,
Then war would end and famine cease,
And all the world would live in peace.

If ever I should stop and cry,
Or lose my way and wonder why,
I think of you and lose my sad,
You transform glumness into glad.

If ever time should stop and stand,
And hourglasses freeze with sand,
For all of time would be on view,
The precious love I hold for you.

If ever age should bow my limb,
Or illness take a wayward trim,
Then my last breath would shout anew,
I truly loved, because of you.

In the first line, how do I describe my love?
What do I say would 'cease'?
What is transformed into 'glad'?
What might happen to hourglasses if time stopped?
What might cause a 'wayward trim'?
What could make me 'wonder why'?

In the first line, how do I describe my love?
Perfect.

What do I say would 'cease'?
Famine.

What is transformed into 'glad'?
Glumness.

What might happen to hourglasses if time stopped?
They would freeze with sand.

What might cause a 'wayward trim'?
Illness.

What could make me 'wonder why'?
Losing my way.

Imagine placing a two-sided mirror on the dashed vertical line. Can you draw what you would see reflected on each side of the mirror?

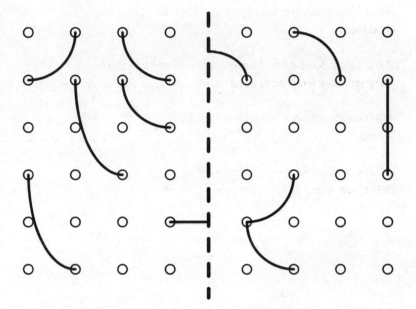

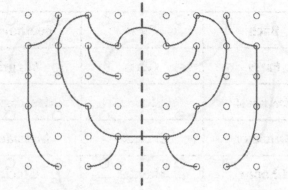

Word Order

Look at the following list of composers for up to one minute.
On the next page you will find the same list but in a different
order. When time is up, turn the page and see how accurately
you can recall the original position of each of the words.

Bach	**Byrd**	**Beethoven**
Parry	**Glass**	**Allegri**
Tchaikovsky	**Strauss**	**Mussorgsky**
Bruckner	**Grainger**	**Messiaen**
Chopin	**Handel**	**Gluck**

Missing Words

Once you have completed the above task, try this one too.
Study these two lists of related words for one minute, then turn
the page and try to spot which word is missing from each list.

**orange   banana   kumquat   peach
pear   nectarine   kiwi**

**minute   eon   millisecond   year
eternity   moment   fortnight**

Word Order

Try to place the composers back in their original boxes:

Chopin	**Allegri**	**Strauss**
Gluck	**Bach**	**Byrd**
Bruckner	**Glass**	**Beethoven**
Grainger	**Mussorgsky**	**Parry**
Messiaen	**Handel**	**Tchaikovsky**

Now turn back to the previous page for the second task.

Missing Words

Can you spot which word is missing from each list?

peach   pear   nectarine _____
banana   kiwi   orange

year   millisecond   moment _____
minute   fortnight   eternity

Now turn back to check your answer.

Mentally rearrange and join together the 9 square tiles below in order to reveal a hidden letter or number. Don't rotate or mirror any of the tiles.

What is revealed?

A letter 'W' is revealed.

How many bricks can you count in the 3-dimensional arrangement below? Each brick is a perfect cube and the arrangement was created by starting with a 5 by 4 by 6 cuboid of bricks and then removing some bricks. You should assume that all hidden bricks – those obscured by other bricks – are still present.

There are 76 cubes – by level from the top down there are 7, 6, 15, 18, 16 and 14 respectively.

For each of the following totals, choose just 1 number from each ring of this dartboard so that those 4 numbers add up to the given total. For example, you would form a total of 19 by picking 3, 12, 1 and 3 from the outer- to the innermost rings respectively.

41

77

83

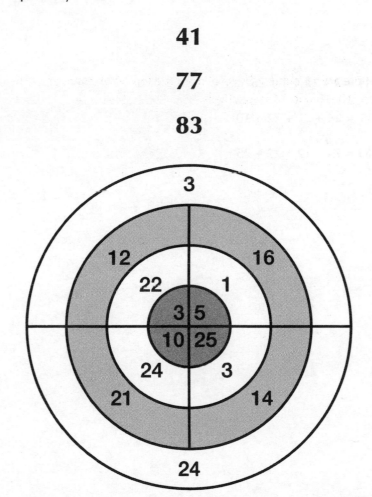

41 = 3 + 12 + 1 + 25

77 = 24 + 21 + 22 + 10

83 = 24 + 12 + 22 + 25

Study the shaded circles for no more than 30 seconds, then cover them over and answer the questions beneath.

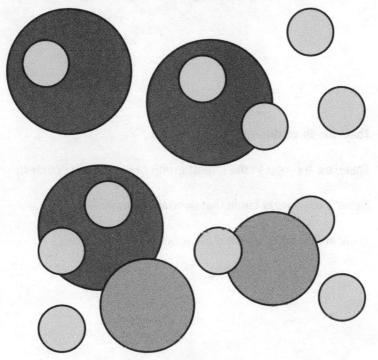

How many different sizes of circle are there?

In total, how many circles are there in the largest group of overlapping circles?

How many bigger circles are there that overlap a smaller circle?

And how many circles are there which do not touch any other circles at any point?

There are three different sizes of circle.

There are 4 circles in the largest group of overlapping circles.

There is one bigger circle that overlaps a smaller circle.

There are 4 circles which don't touch any other circles.

BRAIN CHAINS

How quickly can you solve each of the following brain chains? Without making any written notes, start with the number on the left and follow the arrows while applying each operation in turn. Write the result in the empty box at the end.

| 213 | +267 | -433 | Add three hundred and twenty-six | -191 | RESULT |

| 364 | +50 | One half of this | -58 | ×4 | RESULT |

| 254 | +50% | +146 | ÷17 | Add four hundred and thirty-eight | RESULT |

| 396 | ÷18 | +297 | Subtract forty-four | +296 | RESULT |

| 236 | +50% | -110 | +88 | -92 | RESULT |

The results are: 182
596
469
571
240

By drawing along the existing lines, can you divide this shape up into 4 identical jigsaw pieces, with no pieces left over? The pieces may be rotated versions of one another, but you cannot mirror or 'turn over' any of the pieces.

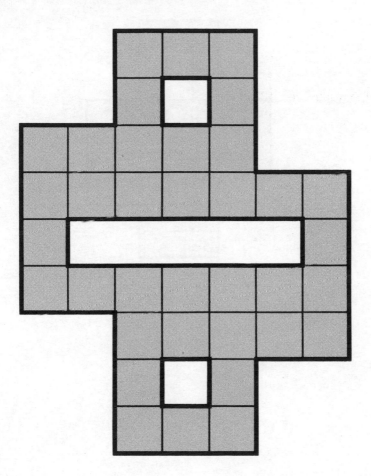

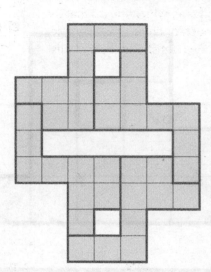

SHAPE LINK

Can you connect each pair of identical shapes together by drawing only horizontal and vertical lines from square to square? No more than one line can enter each square, which means that the lines can't touch or cross. The example solution on the right should help clarify the rules.

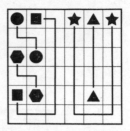

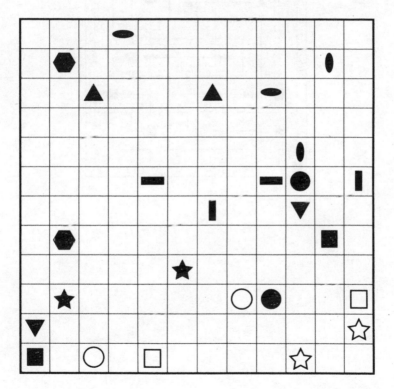

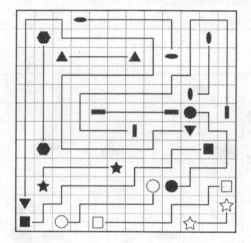

Draw solid lines along some of the dashed lines in order to
divide the grid up into a set of rectangles, so that every number
is inside only one rectangle. The number inside each rectangle
must be exactly equal to the number of grid squares that the
rectangle contains.

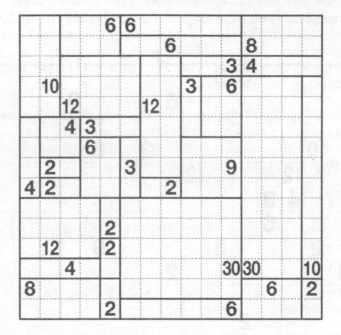

*Read the following passage and then answer the questions below **without** referring back to the text. Once you have answered as many questions as you can, read the text a second time and see if you can then answer all the remaining questions.*

Once upon a time there was a journey. The journey became a story, and with time the twists and turns of adventure became legend. As the years passed the legends fell into myth, and the heroes became gods who walked among the people as monuments to greatness.

In every telling, the tales of daring adventure, death in foreign lands and love against the odds grew and grew. One lover became a hundred more, and every fierce creature grew horns and wings and scales. Each rock-face breathed fire, and every ocean seethed with the bubbling torment of a million deadly creatures.

And so the myth grew, and the people who once walked with the gods fell into fear, and declined.

Before the journey evolved into legend, what was it in the years between?

What had the heroes become once the journey became myth?

What do I say there was 'once upon a time'?

What is it said 'became a hundred more'?

Where was death said to occur?

With time, what did every rock-face start to do?

And what did the oceans start to seethe with?

Before the journey evolved into legend, what was it in the years between?
A story.

What had the heroes become once the journey became myth?
Gods who walked among the people.

What do I say there was 'once upon a time'?
A journey.

What is it said 'became a hundred more'?
One lover.

Where was death said to occur?
Foreign lands.

With time, what did every rock-face start to do?
Breathe fire.

And what did the oceans start to seethe with?
A million deadly creatures.

Mentally join together the nine square tiles below in order to reveal a simple hidden picture. You will need to rotate some or all of the tiles, but do not mirror (or 'flip over') any of them.

What is revealed?

A picture of a hand is revealed.

Given the following set of numbers and mathematical signs, can you rearrange them to obtain the given result?

You must use all of the numbers and signs, but you can use as many additional 'brackets' as you like.

For example, (4×3) − (2×5) = 2.

$$3 \quad\quad 3 \quad\quad 12 \quad\quad 25 \quad\quad 50$$
$$+ \quad\quad + \quad\quad \times \quad\quad \div$$

RESULT: 19

Now try to do the same with this set too:

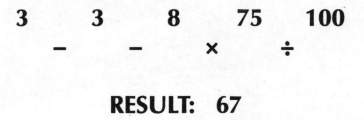

$$3 \quad\quad 3 \quad\quad 8 \quad\quad 75 \quad\quad 100$$
$$- \quad\quad - \quad\quad \times \quad\quad \div$$

RESULT: 67

$$(((25 + 50) \times 3) + 3) \div 12 = \mathbf{19}$$

$$(((100 - 8) \times 3) - 75) \div 3 = \mathbf{67}$$

Draw solid lines along some of the dashed lines in order to divide the grid up into a set of rectangles, so that every number is inside only one rectangle. The number inside each rectangle must be exactly equal to the number of grid squares that the rectangle contains.

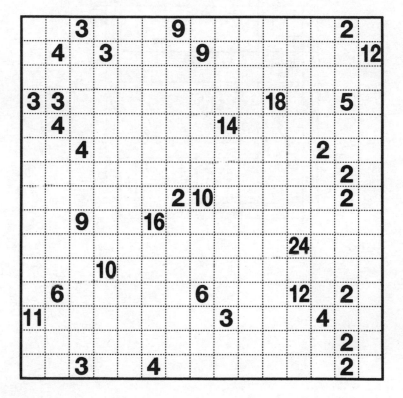

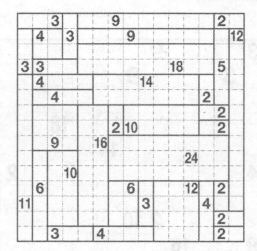

Which of these is the odd one out, and why?

C	L	D
X	K	V

What number comes next in this mathematical sequence?

3   7   19   55   163   487   _____

And which letter comes next in this sequence?

A   B   D   O   P   Q   _____

If I toss a coin 3 times, what is the likelihood it lands on tails 2 or more times?

_____

If **DOG** goes to **FQI**, and **CAT** goes to **ECV**, what does **FISH** go to?

_____

If I photograph a sugar cube that has been placed on a table, what is the maximum number of corners I can see on the cube in that photo, assuming there are no mirrors?

_____

How many odd-numbered pages are there in this book? Only count those pages which have page numbers at the bottom.

_____

Look at the following list of synonyms and spend up to one minute trying to memorize all 9 words. Then turn the page and recall as many as possible.

Finish	Complete	Culminate	End	Achieve
Fulfil	Attain	Stop	Accomplish	

Which of these words is the odd one out, and why?
K – all of the rest are Roman numerals.

What number comes next in this mathematical sequence?
1459. At each step twice the value of one less than the previous number is added.

And which letter comes next in this sequence?
R. These are the capital letters with enclosed spaces in them, from A to Z.

If I toss a coin 3 times, what is the likelihood it lands on tails 2 or more times?
1 in 2.

If DOG goes to FQI, and CAT goes to ECV, what does FISH go to?
HKUJ. Each new letter is two later in the alphabet.

If I photograph a sugar cube that has been placed on a table, what is the maximum number of corners I can see on the cube in that photo, assuming there are no mirrors?
7 corners.

How many odd-numbered pages are there in this book? Only count those pages which have page numbers at the bottom.
93. The first odd page with a number on is page 7 and the last is 191, so there are 93 odd-numbered pages.

Recall the synonyms:

Spend no more than one minute studying the top picture.
When time is up, cover it over and redraw it as accurately as
you can on the empty grid below.

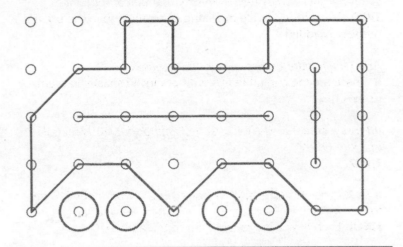

Now try to redraw the same image on this blank page. You can turn back and study it for as long as you like before attempting this task.

By drawing along the existing lines, can you divide this shape up into 4 identical jigsaw pieces, with no pieces left over? The pieces may be rotated versions of one another, but you cannot mirror or 'turn over' any of the pieces.

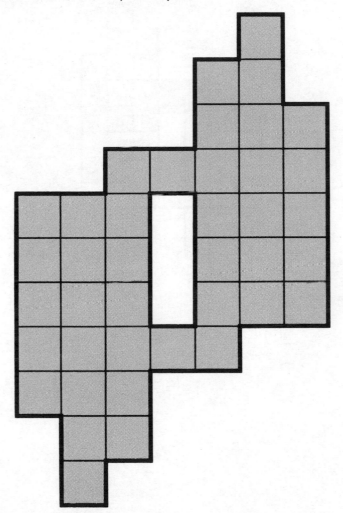

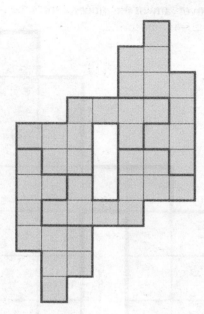

For each of the following totals, choose just 1 number from each ring of this dartboard so that those 3 numbers add up to the given total. For example, you would form a total of 39 by picking 17 from the outermost ring, 12 from the middle ring and 10 from the innermost ring.

50

58

74

81

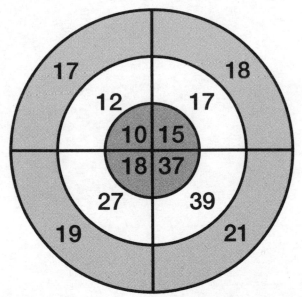

50 = 18 + 17 + 15

58 = 21 + 27 + 10

74 = 17 + 39 + 18

81 = 17 + 27 + 37

Can you redraw the top picture on the bottom grid while rotating it a quarter turn (90 degrees) anti-clockwise, as indicated by the arrow? Try to do this without rotating the book at all! Once done, it will reveal a hidden message.

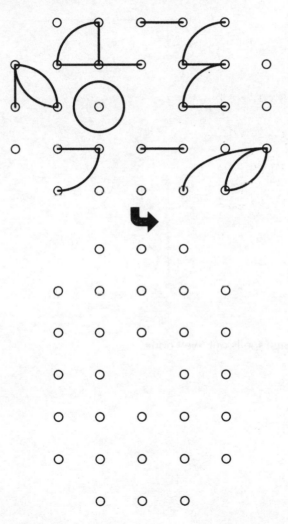

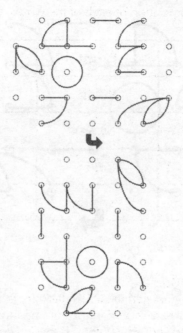

The image spells out 'well done'.

Word Order

Look at the following list of birds for up to one minute. On the next page you will find the same list but in a different order. When time is up, turn the page and see how accurately you can recall the original position of each of the words.

Curlew	**Parrot**	**Puffin**
Duck	**Robin**	**Raven**
Kite	**Swan**	**Linnet**
Magpie	**Turkey**	**Owl**
Budgerigar	**Penguin**	**Osprey**

Missing Words

Once you have completed the above task, try this one too. Study these two lists of related words for one minute, then turn the page and try to spot which word is missing from each list.

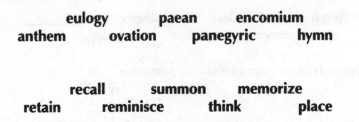

eulogy   **paean**   **encomium**
anthem   **ovation**   **panegyric**   **hymn**

recall   **summon**   **memorize**
retain   **reminisce**   **think**   **place**

Word Order

Try to place the birds back in their original boxes:

Owl	Turkey	Robin
Osprey	Raven	Kite
Swan	Magpie	Puffin
Budgerigar	Linnet	Duck
Penguin	Curlew	Parrot

Now turn back to the previous page for the second task.

Missing Words

Can you spot which word is missing from each list?

hymn	ovation	anthem	_____
	encomium	paean	eulogy

reminisce	memorize	summon	_____
	retain	place	recall

Now turn back to check your answer.

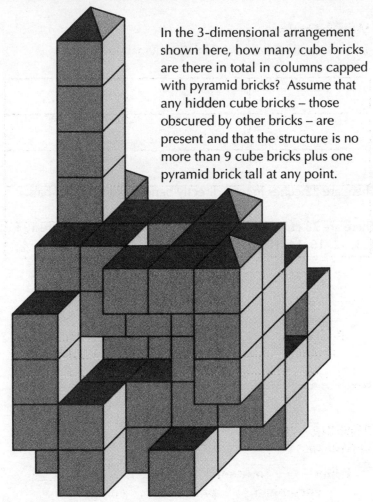

In the 3-dimensional arrangement shown here, how many cube bricks are there in total in columns capped with pyramid bricks? Assume that any hidden cube bricks – those obscured by other bricks – are present and that the structure is no more than 9 cube bricks plus one pyramid brick tall at any point.

And how many cube bricks are there in the arrangement in total? The arrangement was created by starting with a 5 by 4 by 9 cuboid of bricks and then removing some bricks. Then once complete pyramid shapes were added on top of some columns of bricks – do not count these. You should assume that all hidden cube bricks are still present.

There are 22 cubes in total directly beneath the pyramid hats.

There are 78 cubes – by level from the top down there are 1, 1, 1, 1, 12, 16, 14, 17 and 15 respectively.

Study the 3 different sizes of pointed shape below for 30 seconds, then cover them over and answer the questions beneath.

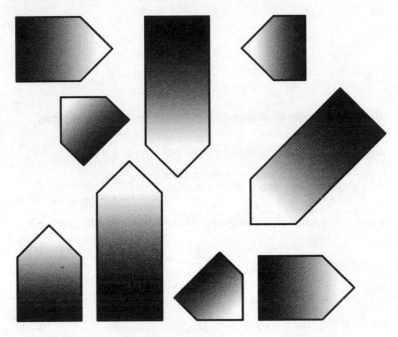

How many pairs of shapes of identical orientation and size are there?

What is the total number of shapes?

How many shapes point both down and to the left?

And how many shapes point upwards (including both straight up, and up and to one side)?

There is one pair of shapes of identical orientation and size.

There are 9 shapes in total.

One shape points down and to the left.

There are 3 shapes pointing upward or upward and to one side.

SHAPE LINK

Can you connect each pair of identical shapes together by drawing only horizontal and vertical lines from square to square? No more than one line can enter each square, which means that the lines can't touch or cross. The example solution on the right should help clarify the rules.

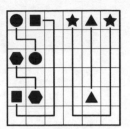

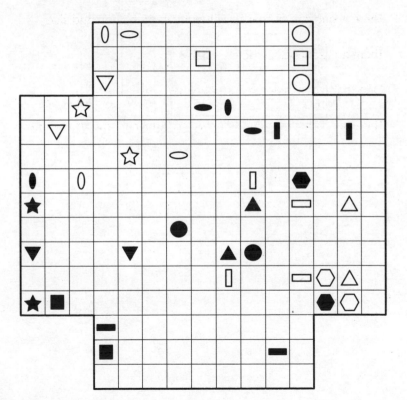

SHAPE LINK

BRAIN CHAINS

How quickly can you solve each of the following brain chains?
Without making any written notes, start with the number on
the left and follow the arrows while applying each operation in
turn. Write the result in the empty box at the end.

| 292 | ÷2 | +333 | -292 | +23 | RESULT |

| 123 | +402 | ÷15 | +394 | 1/3 of this | RESULT |

| 398 | 1/2 of this | -159 | +10% | +335 | RESULT |

| 54 | +366 | ÷3 | +30% | +177 | RESULT |

| 281 | +461 | -298 | ÷3 | +332 | RESULT |

The results are: 210
                  143
                  379
                  359
                  480

The same picture is shown here twice, but in each case different parts of it have been hidden behind dark grey tiles. By imagining combining the two images in your head, can you answer the following questions?

How many separate shapes are there?

How many sides does the shape with the most sides have?

And how many sides does the shape with the fewest sides have?

There are 3 shapes.

There are 15 sides on the shape with the most sides (the centre shape).

The shape with least sides has 9 sides (the bottom shape).

The combined image looks like this:

*Read the following poem as slowly as you like and then answer
the questions below **without** referring back to the text. Once
you have answered as many questions as you can, see how
many you can answer after a second reading, and so on.*

If ever a tale was made to tell,
Life would be it, from dip to swell.
Of good and bad we'd speak it all,
Verdant promise and bitter fall.

Each day adventure breaks anew,
Stories mixed in life's great stew,
Always onward, never back,
Rumbling down a twisted track.

And if some days the journey's slow,
Sudden congestion won't let us go,
Even then we know it's true,
Hope remains; each breath is new.

Dream greatly; wander wide;
Explore always: tales to tell.

Venture on.
                    Forever.

What 'breaks anew' each day?
What is it that sometimes won't 'let us go'?
In what is it said that stories are mixed?
What two-word phrase is contrasted with 'bitter fall'?
What is it said that life is 'rumbling down'?
What is said to 'remain', even when the journey is slow?

What 'breaks anew' each day?
Adventure.

What is it that sometimes won't 'let us go'?
Congestion.

In what is it said that stories are mixed?
Life's great stew.

What two-word phrase is contrasted with 'bitter fall'?
Verdant promise.

What is it said that life is 'rumbling down'?
A twisted track.

What is said to 'remain', even when the journey is slow?
Hope.